Sin, Sacrifice, Heaven & Hell

RAY SHORTELL

ISBN: 0692869379
ISBN-13: 978-0-692-86937-6

DEDICATION

For Dad and all those who wonder whether there is more to life.

CONTENTS

ACKNOWLEDGMENTS

Robert Eisenman is awesome!

1 PRELUDE: THE END OF ISRAEL - SALT OF THE EARTH

Romans used the following scriptures to justify/document the destruction of Israel:

Thou sawest till that a stone was cut out without hands, which smote the image upon his feet that were of iron and clay, and brake them to pieces. Then was the iron, the clay, the brass, the silver, and the gold, broken to pieces together, and became like the chaff of the summer threshingfloors; and the wind carried them away, that no place was found for them: and the stone that smote the image became a great mountain, and filled the whole earth.
Daniel 2:34 – 35

Daniel was probably written in Roman times and refers to the modern Jewish view of resurrection (modern: roughly 40 CE and not necessarily commonly accepted among Jews today). While probably originally intended to support Jewish rulership of the world, noting Jerusalem centered in the middle of three continents, I believe Rome turned this scripture upon its ear to justify the destruction of Israel. Rome intended to remove temple sacrifice from the face of the earth, finding both animal sacrifice and circumcision abhorrent. The intent was to replace Judaism with Christianity as espoused by Paul, who noted: And every priest standeth daily ministering and offering oftentimes the same sacrifices which can never take away sins: (Heb 10:11). Daniel's metaphor gets interpreted with Peter referenced in my opinion as Daniel's rock <above> as per Peter's nickname, Cephas (a hollowed-out rock):

...Simon Peter answered and said: Thou art the Christ, the Son of the living G-d. And Jesus answered and said ... Thou art Peter (or Cephas, a stone per Jn 1:42), and upon this rock I will build my church. And I will give thee the keys to the kingdom of heaven ...
Matthew 16:16 – 19

Paul and the gospels go to great lengths explaining that the second covenant, not based upon temple sacrifice or even at Jerusalem, the covenant of the fleshly heart, has superseded, according to him, the antiquated covenant of Moses as anticipated by Eze 11:19, heart of flesh and Hosea 6:6 mercy and not sacrifice. Paul references several Hebraic scriptural instances of the promise carried by the second son (Esau, Ishmael - Ro 9:7, 12-13).

...ye are manifestly declared to be the epistle of Christ ministered by us, written not in tables with ink, but with the Spirit of the living G-d; not in tables of stone, but in fleshy tables of the heart...these are the two covenants; the one from Mt. Sinai (in Arabia) which gendereth unto bondage... Jerusalem... with her children... But Jerusalem which is above is free, which is the mother of us all. Cast out the bondwoman and her son.
2 Cor 3:3,6-7

So the last shall be first and the first last... Mt 20:16

Ye shall not worship in Jerusalem but shall worship in spirit and truth. Jn 4:23

But if ye had known what this meaneth, I will have mercy, and not sacrifice, ye would not have condemned the guiltless. Mt 12:7 on Ho 6:6

And so begins the story of how Rome justified taxing, dispossessing, and sending the remnant of Israel enslaved to build the Coliseum in Rome, using temple gold to pay guards (1). Romans destroyed the temple and ransacked Jews in cities around the Mediterranean, as per the historian Josephus. Rome took the temple ornaments, removing temple sacrifice from earth. In 300 CE, bishop Eusebius relished the destruction, blaming Jerusalem for the crucifixion (2). Eusebius' records are essential due to a dearth of previous records, many having been burned as "heretical," just as Rome burned the library of Alexandria (3). Paul, the gospels, and Paul's posthumous writings continue the bloodthirsty prosecution/justification of Roman vengeance:

For if they which are of the law be heirs, faith is made void, and the promise made of none effect. Ro 4:14.

...the blood of all the prophets, which was shed from the foundation of the world, may be required of this generation; From the blood of Able unto the blood of Zacharias which perished between the altar and the temple: Verily I say unto you, It shall be required of this generation. Luke 11:50-51

Then answered all the people, and said, His blood be on us, and on our children. Mt 27:25

...the Jews. Who both killed the Lord Jesus, and their own prophets, and have persecuted us; and they please not G-d and are contrary to all men: I Thes 2:14-15.

The above blood libel claim is most famous, ringing down from the ages, based upon the crucifixion of Jesus. However, other scriptures also come to life given the light of Roman vengeance for Jewish failure to pay the tax, scriptures previously indiscernible: *Ye are the salt of the earth: but if the salt has lost his savor, wherewith shall it be salted? It is thenceforth good for nothing but to be cast out and trodden under foot of men. Mt 5:13, Mk 9:50, Lk 14:34-35*

This parable was previously undiscernible because salt does not lose its savor. Salt is sodium and chlorine. The ionic bond between sodium and chlorine does not come apart even in water. In my opinion, salt trodden underfoot is a reference to the use of salt in the fields of Shechem, where Judah sewed it into farmers' fields to prevent Samaritans from ever again raising an army (Judges 9:45). Christians, therefore, have become "the salt of the earth" designed never to allow Jerusalem to rise from her ashes. As Jesus notes - *Jerusalem will be trodden down underfoot by the Gentiles until the times of the Gentiles be fulfilled. Lk 21:24*

Paul's analogy regarding Christians being the aroma of sweetness to those in Christ and the aroma of death to those outside the fold (II Cor 2:15) may likewise have portentous intimations for Jerusalem much like perdition awaiting wayward Christians (Heb 10:29).

And there is (Mt 21:33-46, Mk 12:1-11, Lk 20:1-19) the parable of the owner (G-d) who sends his servants (the prophets) to sharecroppers (the temple authority) for the payment of season. Finally, the owner sends his Son (Jesus) to request payment, who the sharecroppers abuse and kill. Jesus has the scribes propose: *...He (G-d) will miserably destroy those wicked men (the temple authority)... Mt 21:41* noting *Mk 11:17: ...ye have made it (the temple) a den of thieves...* and *Mk 12:9: What shall therefore the lord of the vineyard do? He will come and destroy the husbandmen (sharecroppers) and will give the vineyard (Israel) unto others.* Afterward, Jesus interprets his "rock" as pulverizing the temple authorities.

Or as Jesus says in Lk 19:27 (as author Sam Harris notes) regarding the servants (Christians) of the City (the Spiritual Jerusalem), who fail to proselytize effectively by bringing new members into the fold, or even more so, the temple authority for failing to recognize the authority of Jesus: *But those mine enemies, which would not that I should reign over them, bring hither, and slay them before me.*

Could any Roman soldier not take this message to heart while serving? Could any Roman officer be unwilling to present such scriptures to any soldier wishing to preserve historic ruins or avoid breaking the sixth commandment against killing? Should the Roman Catholic Church be held accountable for setting a context justifying murder, genocide, confiscation, and annexation down through the ages, including the German Holocaust, in the name of the almighty?

2 FOREWORD: UNDERSTANDING THE BIBLE

My first book was fantastic, but Dad said to write another, and I wondered how to do it better. It had to cover a history of the development of Catholic Theology fraught with the deaths of heretics and the persecution of Jews. Yet this second book also needed to cover origins and what we can glean from the beginning of our era through the prism of two millennia. My first book was for people with little time to read, but this second is more in-depth. My feeling is, as Jesus proposed, that no one should feel inferior or lacking information when discussing religion with whoever are our scribes, lawyers, and doctors of the law (Lk 11:46). Whereas my first book described Rome's destructiveness, from which we get the word "decimate," this second covers how Rome used the lessons of the past (Carthage) to utterly destroy Israel's temple-centered religion as described in Mt 5:13, the metaphor of salt trodden underfoot.

This book reviews sin, asking whether you believe sin can destroy your relationship with our creator. This book asks about heaven and hell seeking whether you believe in an eternal reward and punishment or that the creator of both would lock the gates of heaven or the gates of hell to remove any of creation from itself (sic). This book asks about sacrifice and forgiveness, asking how pain for an innocent animal or person or donations to charity might make amends for transgression outside of a human social context towards the author of creation. This book reviews Jesus, his contempt for academia, and his rejection of "the world," apparently including temple bankers, lawyers, scribes, Pharisees, Sadducees, doctors of the law, towns deserving of hellfire, and fruitless fig trees. This book reviews Paul's dim view of those who resisted his (sic) gospel. This book reviews the biblical conviction that one day, we should all be priests, rulers, angels, or g-ds, depending upon your translation. Biblical authors claim that we will be like them one day, needing no intercessor between ourselves and our creator. Finally, this book asks when you believe this might happen.

Thesis: Sin, Sacrifice, Heaven, and Hell provides a short synopsis of the author's previous work, "Understanding the Bible", before seeking our place in the kingdom with a biblical review of sin, sacrifice, heaven, and hell. Additional chapters include doctrines of Catholics and atheists humbly seeking to thwart any claiming authority or exclusive access to ineffable information. We have too many biblical translations in this age of information and enlightenment for a priest to be able to claim any longer that one must learn five different languages to be able to correctly interpret the Bible (St. Michael's Woodstock GA Fr Michael ~2004) thereby effectively quashing discussion, while simultaneously declaring the Church demands of followers: obedience and humility. With the Catholic Church, as per the Bible, it is easy to be a follower, yet there are many methods of enrolling conformity and eliminating dissent.

Notably, the author translates "conscupience" (Ro 7:8) as [the law brought my conscience to bear upon my base desires and spiritual yearnings]. This single word sums up Paul's view on sin and how, in Paul's opinion, those who have not heard of grace find an inner imperfection through "the laws of nature." Note: I've taken a bit of liberty with Paul's words in I Cor. 11:14, as per Ro 2:14, arriving at "the laws of nature," which carry the same meaning, purposefully reordered into the words from our American Declaration of Independence, much as others have correctly reordered Paul's words proposing: "The letter of the law brings death" (Ro 7:6).

For a quick review of my previous book:

Rome destroyed everything (1). Rome intended a Jewish genocide in Israel, Alexandria, and throughout the Mediterranean but enslaved and ordered thousands to Rome to build the Coliseum (2). Until the temple's destruction in 70, there was an annual Jewish pilgrimage to Jerusalem, which some undertook only once (Crucifixion and Turin Shroud Mysteries Solved Pierre Krijbolder 1976, 1989, 1999 p106). Rome destroyed the temple in 70 and Massada in 72. Herod beheaded John the Baptist in 37 and crucified Jesus in 40 (my opinion). Paul murdered Jacob (James) in 62, with the subsequent Jewish tax revolt erupting in 66.

Josephus, the turncoat Jewish head of the northern (Galilean) defense, details the carnage and confiscation of property at cities in Israel and around the Mediterranean in Wars and Antiquities, memoirs authored from Rome(3).

Later in the first century or early in the next, Rome continued its genocide, seeking any remaining of the Davidic line, such as the grandchildren of Jude, who had requested the Syrian bishopric as rightful heirs. Jesus, not the oldest of four or five brothers and at least two sisters (4), went willingly to the cross as his family's sacrifice, as a Mafioso proof of loyalty (my opinion). Jacob (James), Jesus' older brother, was therefore allowed to continue to preach at the temple in Jerusalem for another twenty years, vegetarian and celibate, continually recounting his brother's sacrifice. Roman sympathizer Paul figuratively destroyed everything pointing to temple supremacy - the genealogy and lineage including that of Jacob, the temple sacrifice, the holy of holies, the years of studying including languages (Jerusalem having multitudinous visitors being in the middle of three continents), the food, the circumcision, the festivals, the law, essentially destroying anything not contained in Paul's word "freedom". Paul's virtues are primarily of faith, while Jacob's virtues are primarily of works. Jacob died in Jerusalem in 62, apparently during Paul's last recorded moments in Acts, while he was ostensibly in Rome, with his stated intention of continuing onto Spain, which may have merely been an alibi (Dr. Eisenman suggests that Paul may have been in Jerusalem leading the death of Jacob, noting that Paul's presence in Jerusalem tended to create riots. At the same time, Jacob lived there peaceably - Billy Graham's book THE MESSAGE references Jacob as "old camel knees" for his many hours in prayer at the temple).

The Essenes believe money violates the second commandment against graven images because it includes a picture of Caesar and the Jewish law for not having anyone other than a brother as king. In my opinion, the Essenes, therefore, lived in a cashless society. Their dim view of money is present in I Timothy 6:10, which calls the love of money the root of all evil, and in Matthew, which notes serving either G-d or "mammon". Anytime the Bible chooses an "interesting" word for something, you can be sure something is afoot, for example, the words "Didymus" meaning "Twin", and either "Dioscuri" or "Heavenly twins" meaning "Gemini," with "Mazaroth" meaning "Signs of the Zodiac" ("Zoo"-diac). "Living water" is another exciting word explained in this book. You'll remember from the Bible that only one disciple held the money (Judas - Jn 13:9). Neither Jesus nor the other disciples, except Peter for the temple tax, touched the money. Perhaps Judas washed each night like a priest coming in from a sacrifice (Num 19:7). Probably among the Essenes, no one held any money at all (archaeologists having trouble finding coins(5)). Roman tax collectors had a tough time collecting from vegetarian Essenes living in a common room, each prizing a sole linen robe, a communal sword or two as per Peter's "here are two" (Lk 22:38), and cold bath in the morning. Perhaps Romans took over some properties in lieu. Acts 5:2 references a disciple's property where "the apostles" take charge of the sale. Mt 5:40 says that if a man legally takes your cloak, you should also give him your coat. Mt 10:10 suggests not having two coats. Rome would probably confiscate the second in place of the tax. Dr. Eisenman notes one of the charges laid against Jesus at his trial was that he told people not to pay their taxes (Lk 23:2). The Essenes or "The Poor" (Gal 2:10) eschewed money like Jesus who threw the money-changers (bankers) out of the temple (Jn 2:15). Jesus neither touched nor worked for and did not contribute to the economic system for the coin, which he used to pay the temple-tax. Jesus never personally violated the second commandment, even according to the law of the Essenes (Mt 17:27), which leads to the question of who received the temple tax (Priests? Herod? Rome?). Dr. Eisenman describes the War as starting with a tax revolt (6).

Per Acts, the Jews of Asia accused Paul of bringing Greeks into the temple (7)(Trophimus the Ephesian - Acts 21:29, Acts 20:4, II Tim 4:20) - for instance, in addition to other Greeks at Paul's church of Antioch, Paul's disciple Timothy (Paul's "son" in the faith I Tim 1:2) had a Greek father and Jewish mother (Acts 16:3). Stephen, another disciple at Antioch with a Greek name meaning crowned or king, presents an odd portrait: Paul, supposedly the apostle to the gentiles, instigates the stoning of a Stephen at the temple (Acts

7:58). Who might have been this Stephen's evangelist? Who might have given Paul the authority to stone another? The gospels, written in Greek after most or all of the letters of Paul, support Paul's position (I Tim 1:4, Tit 3:9) with Jesus proposing instead of Jews, raising stones as heirs to Abraham (Mt 3:9), noting "the Jews" as not acting like the descendants of Abraham (Jn 8:39). Wine is a homonym of Greek per Dr. Eisenman. Jesus proclaimed that you don't put new wine into old wineskins (foreskins, both referencing sacrifice in my opinion) (Mt 9:17) and turned water in the stone jars into wine, meaning that Greeks don't need to be circumcised. Paul's previous rants against circumcision, pre-dating the gospels, are in Phil 3:2, I Cor 7:19, Gal 5:2, 6, 6:13. Simultaneously these imply the temple authorities as, pardon the obscenity, "old saggy sacks" (old wineskins Mt 9:17). Meanwhile, contradicting his own words regarding freedom, Paul had Timothy circumcised to allow him to preach in synagogues (Acts 16:3).

****************************Follow-up:**************************

Per Pierre Krijbolder's Crucifixion and Turin Shroud Mysteries Solved 1976, 1989, 1999, pg 200, the reference to "stone jars" may have been a reference to Peter, aka "Cephas." In my opinion, playing with the words "rock" or "stones" (Lk 3:8), as in raising children unto Abraham from stones, may reference male anatomy, in light of Jesus referencing the temple authority as "old saggy sacks," by which Jesus may have been deriding circumcision.

Per Pierre Krijbolder pg 30, the words for "old wineskin" and "leprous" were the same due to their similar appearance. Obviously, Jesus was referencing the temple authority, which in my opinion might mean that when Jesus was healing "lepers," he was converting Sadducees... but that's a stretch.

Finally, this follow-up tells the story of the woman at the well. As one man has said, when you drink the water, remember who dug the well (Justin Sterling of the Sterling Institute of Relationship). The woman references Jacob (Israel) as having dug the well. The woman is Samaritan, whom the Jews despised. Per Josephus Antiquities 9.14.3, Samaritans sometimes claimed to be Jews, when it suited their purposes. At other times when the Jews were in danger from Rome, Samaritans would disavow the Jews. Jesus continues "telling her all she ever did" by marrying several people and finally shacking up with a man. Jesus suggests his "living water" instead, noting that afterward, she would never need to return to the well (Jn 4:5-13).

In my opinion, this story explains that the good wine in stone jars represented Greeks (Romans), that the living water came from Jacob (Jews, Torah), and that raising descendants to Abraham from rocks was Jesus saying, like Paul, that we are the true descendants. "And all did drink of the same spiritual drink: for they drank of that spiritual Rock that followed them: and that Rock was Christ" (I Cor 10:4). As the wine steward proposed: ...thou hast kept the good wine until now (Jn 2:10).

*********************End of Follow-up**************************

Regarding the laws that Paul and Jesus rewrote, note that Jesus followed the law to the letter, specifically not touching money while supporting his disciples in Paul's word, "freedom." Remember that Paul's writings pre-dated the gospels. Paul noted his freedom from the law of eating (I Cor 6:12), which Jesus professed but never violated in the gospels (Mt 15:1-20). Similarly, Jesus' disciples worked on the Sabbath (Mt 12:1-13), which Jesus allowed while meticulously following the letter of the law himself. Paul's mention of the Sabbath in Col 2:16 says we might be just fine not esteeming one day above others. Jesus notes the Sabbath as a servant to people rather than people as servants to the Sabbath (Lk 13:15) and the Sabbath as a day where it is ok to get your ass out of a pit (yes, it says that, pardon my fourteen-year-old humor, Lk 14:5). Paul's church of Antioch where Christianity was first named (Acts 11:26), finds Greeks upset with table service for widows before Paul's conversion (Acts 6:1), lists Herod's foster brother as an esteemed member (Acts 13:1), and frees people from everything associated with temple worship, even promoting fraternization between Greeks and Jews (Gal 2:12).

Paul who was Roman and probably Herodian was of no mean city (Acts 21:39), had a nephew who collected the Roman guard at one of Paul's riots in Jerusalem (Acts 23:16-24), essentially hid in Herod's

Caesarea (Acts 9:30, Acts 25), and had a foster brother of Herod at his church in Antioch (Acts 13:1). Paul had Roman support in beating the leader of the Synagogue in Corinth (Acts 18:17). Per Dr. Eisenman, Corinth was Caesar's summer home and governed by Galio (Acts 18:17), who was brother to Caesar's secretary, both being from Spain (Paul's last writings note Spain as his intended destination Ro 15:24, 28). Finally, Paul greets "the brothers" in Rome (Acts 28:14,15 - who were their evangelists?) and notes a young Herodian in Rome as a near kinsman (Ro 16:11).

Rome kept the temple garments of the high priest and chose each succeeding high priest.

For both Paul and Jacob (James), the big question was how to pacify the power of Rome. James, of the lineage of kings & priests like his brother, Jesus (Lk 1:36-40), lived in Jerusalem preaching, teaching, and praying for peace for twenty years after the sacrifice of Jesus (Jacob died in 62 at the age of 96 per Josephus Antiquities 20.9.1). Paul chose direct support of Roman ideals using metaphors grounded in Roman sports (naked Olympic wrestling and running in races 12.5.1 Antiquities, Josephus), privily spying on circumcisions which Romans considered castration (Rome occasionally referencing Jews as eunuchs (8)). Paul seems to have purposefully enraged the temple authority. Paul supported paying taxes, not revolting, and never innovating by having peasants killing the king. Paul proposed that G-d had put authority in place and that the peaceful life of Christians was never in opposition to just governmental authority or taxes.

The afterward of Understanding the Bible notes pre-existing Egyptian, Babylonian, and Zoroastrian theology, with the lynchpin being a comparison between I Cor 13 and the solar myth of Hercules as re-enacted annually at Paul's hometown of Tarsus, noting this as the sole positive biblical contribution of Paul. The rest of Paul's letters are reactive: I'm free, live by faith, not in the stodgy roles of "some from Jacob (James)," or those who recommend themselves as something. I'm in no wise behind super-apostles. Jesus came to me. My apostleship is to the Gentiles.). To me, the love chapter of I Cor 13 is plagiarism of the highest magnitude, with no source cited. Incidentally, the four creatures around the throne in Rev 4:7 are the four fixed astrological signs (Lion, Bull, Man, Eagle - the snake and eagle representing the scorpion in its lower and higher arcs – p715 Linda Goodman's Love Signs, 1951).

Regarding the details of how the twelve apostles can't be recited: eight share the same names as the four brothers of Jesus with the remaining four pulled from the annals of Roman history - one apostle even named "twin" in two separate languages. Please check my previous book Understanding the Bible, or Jacob (James), the Brother of Jesus by Dr. Robert Eisenman. To Dr. Eisenman we are also indebted for finding Stephen to have been an outlandish story of an uncircumcised Greek preaching to the Jewish high priest, failing to have been immediately killed by Jewish Sicarii, who carried carved knives under their robes to either circumcise or kill those who dared to discuss theology, much like those who threatened Paul's own life as per Acts 23:12. In chapter nine, Jewish History per Stephen, per Dr. Eisenman, Stephen also misses some specific history upon which a Jewish mob would have pounced. Understanding the Bible chapter seven further covers Dr. Eisenman's contention that Philip's Ethiopian would never have been allowed in the temple as either a stranger (foreigner) or eunuch, that there were no Ethiopian eunuchs, and that there was no Ethiopian ruler referred to as "Candace" at the time.

Post-script to the above chapter per Crucifixion and Turin Shroud Mysteries Solved by Pierre Krijbolder 1976

Christians were Essean - there was a translation issue between Issya and Jesus p28.

This gift of G-d (Nathanael) may have been: the Essaean doctrine (insight) of the immortality of the individual human soul, whereas the traditional immortality of the soul was believed to be restricted to the collectivity in the form of a continuation of the individual's spirit in the (genetic) posterity p27.

Esseans refrained from swearing, believing that if your word alone was not believable, you were already condemned p101 (Mt 5:33-37). The word Essean means healer (like Jesus) p101. Esseans had an initiation of a year or three in the desert, ergo Jesus' forty-day temptation (my opinion) p102 (Mt 4:1). Mediterranean Jews made a pilgrimage to Jerusalem during the High Holy days, so Peter may have started the Roman congregation without ever visiting Italy p106,108. The word Bethlehem means eating of bread and may refer to gaining knowledge or enlightenment p25. Wine may refer to knowledge transmitted in the local language p29. Fishermen may allegorically refer to "seekers of knowledge" p122, and Rabbis were referred to as `shepherds` p35.

Dr. Eisenman also postulates on what the Dead Sea Scrolls refers to as the "three nets of the devil (Belial)": Fornication, Riches, and Pollution of the Sanctuary. Dr. Eisenman shows the first net (fornication) to be related to niece marriage of the Herodians - Herod marrying his half-sister after having divorced the daughter of King Areatas. According to Josephus, Herod lost an army to King Areatas because Herod's Edomite army abandoned Herod and joined Areatas after feeling sorry for how badly Areatas was losing the battle (???). You'll remember Herod beheaded John the Baptist for telling Herod he couldn't marry his brother's wife (Mt 14:3-4). Herod was Edomite, although Rome considered Herod Jewish. Herod married the last of the Maccabeans, who were the Jewish High Priests, although not of the lineage of Aaron (my sources on this are weak). Herod, fearing Jewish rebellion, killed all the other Maccabeans (possibly recounted in the Bible as the murder of the babies in Bethlehem (Mt 2:16)). Herod also kept the high priest's robes in his fortress on the hill across the gulley from the temple where he would look down at the happenings in the temple, thereby (third net) polluting the sacred sanctuary. Herod's hill was higher — someone built the temple by dragging hewn rock down the temple mount. Additionally, the temple was considered (third net) polluted due to Herod choosing the High Priest and (second net) the temple's support of Roman coinage (third net), which rendered the bust of Caesar (Mt 22:20-21) - the second net of Belial (riches) where the priests may have accepted coins at the temple for Herod (Mt 17:21-24) and failed to support the poor - some say the lower caste priests starved (Josephus, Antiquities 20.8.8). Significantly, Jesus preached on all three nets, too, but for the moment, note Jesus throwing "money-changers" out of the temple (Mt 21:12).

3 FOREWORD: CATHOLIC QUESTIONS

When is the Sabbath?

In 321, the Church issued the following while canonizing the scriptures: Christians shall not "Judaize" by resting on the Sabbath but shall work on that day, resting on Sunday instead.

Why are some songs in Latin?

Throughout the Middle and Modern Ages, the Church continued to preach the liturgy in Latin. In the banner year of 1964, Vatican II changed the liturgy into the "vernacular" (local language). In 380, the Church translated the Bible into Latin called "The Vulgate," while 380 BCE found the Pentatuch (the first five books of the Bible) translated into Greek named "the Septuagint". Authors wrote the Greek Scriptures in Greek, the primary language of Rome, starting with Paul's letters 40 - 150 (Paul's death reported in Rome around 64, but with last writings in 62 as near as I can tell around the time of the death of Jacob (James) (pardon my belief in the crucifixion in 40).

Are there any married priests?

Priests were disallowed from marriage early in church history because the Church didn't want children suing the Church for an inheritance (580 Pope Pelagius II that married clergy not bequeath). We do have a married priest or two: Married ministers of another denomination can bring their entire church into Catholicism, becoming ordained priests.

Why aren't altar girls allowed?

Starting before 1990, when I was in Louisville, my Mom and I sat through a service that had altar girls, who were later authorized by the Church in 1994 (letter of the Congregation of Divine Worship and Discipline of the Sacraments to presidents of episcopal conferences).

What is the Church's position on homosexuality?

The Church has no issue with non-practicing homosexuals, although I've heard the church ask for homosexuals to rat out seminarians, promising no consequences for the rat.

Are there more books in the Catholic Bible?

Calvin excluded seven books from the Protestant Bible: Judith, Tobit, Sirach, Baruch, Wisdom, and First and Second Maccabees. Additionally Martin Luther argued against including the book of Jacob (James). These books include doctrine regarding burial, resurrection, purgatory, alms-giving for the forgiveness of sin, and guardian angels: The book of second Maccabees includes belief in a bodily resurrection, even for those who lose body parts (7:9 - 11). After discovering that some of his dead had sinned in secreting booty from the slain of the enemy, Judas Maccabee prays and offers the temple sacrifice on their behalf (12:42-46), acting on a belief in prayer to release the dead from sin (purgatory), including the prayer of saints who have already died (15:12). Tobit tells of guardian angels (12:12, 8:3) and alms including burying the bereft as forgiving sin (12:8) and refers to those outside of the covenant as "g-dless" (15:33).

Daniel was one of the last books of prophets authored, although describing 500 BCE. Daniel's prophesies occasionally slip into the past tense, which apologetic scholars call the "prophetic tense", and get minute details of Roman rulers prophetically accurate while neglecting to know his Babylonian rulers (1). Perhaps Psalm 110 regarding Melchizedek was also written around 167 BCE by Maccabeans, who may have claimed the priesthood based on faith rather than genealogy (2). The Pentateuch, the books of Moses or Torah, was compiled in Daniel's Babylon (3). At the same time, Isaiah prophesied from Jerusalem and Egypt that Cyrus, Daniel's king, would be setting his throne in Egypt, which happened under Median/Persian armies three generations later after they had incorporated Cyrus' legacy into their larger kingdom (3).

Regarding the Greek Scriptures, Paul's writings were first followed by a list of Matthew's fulfilled prophesies as per Eusebius, which became the foundation around which the Synoptics (Matthew, Mark & Luke) were framed (4). Mark wrote next, followed by Luke's research and gathering of anything he could find. Afterward, someone reworked Matthew, filling out the framework of prophecies with traditional stories of Jesus, but did so poorly and seemingly without an editor (my previous job as a typesetter comes through here). John's gospel represents an independent community's authorship, that may or may not have had access to the other gospels, possibly written in a later generation. John chose seven miracles to tell the story of Jesus becoming the fulfillment of our G-d's presence, believing that the fullness of heaven is immanent and working in our world with little reason for speculation on an afterlife. John was probably authored with knowledge of Paul's writings and the original prophetic timeline of Matthew, to refute Mark's focus on reward only after resurrection. Finally, the book of Revelation was authored and allowed into the canon due to the Gospels' emphasis on reward, with little elsewhere describing paradise (See Chapter 8, Heaven).

5 EDUCATION DENOUNCED BY THE BIBLE

Have you ever noticed how Jesus put down anyone who had studied religion: Lawyers, Doctors of the Law, Scribes, Teachers (Pharisees – Synagogue-centered), and even Zealots (Sadducees – Temple-centered(1))? You may be familiar with one or two verses where Jesus condemns academia. This justification, embedded within our society, allows times like when the Church outlawed literacy. Bumper stickers like "my child beat up your honors student" become praiseworthy, and society reviles those who study to do well as "curve busters."

While the Bible mainly denounces education, there is some biblical justification for study: *The heart of him that hath understanding seeketh knowledge... Prov 15:14, Ask, and it will be given you; knock, and it will be opened unto you. Mt 7:7 If one who is lacking in wisdom asks from G-d, without hesitation, it will be given to him. Ja 1:5 ...delight... in the law of the Lord; ... in his law ... meditate day and night. Ps 1:2 Finally, brethren, whatsoever things are true, whatsoever things are honest, whatsoever things are just, whatsoever things are pure, whatsoever things are lovely, whatsoever things are of good report; if there be any virtue, and if there be any praise, think on these things. Ph. 4:8 Or even: ...work out your own salvation with fear and trembling (Ph 2:12).*

But regarding a formal course of study, the Bible protests loudly: *...much study is a weariness of the flesh. Ecc 12:12 It is the glory of G-d to conceal things. Prov 25:2* The Bible proudly condones book burning in an age with no printing press: *Many of them also which used curious arts brought their books together and burned them before all men: and they counted the price of them and found it fifty thousand pieces of silver. Acts 19:19 The Bible philosophizes regarding those seeking knowledge: Ever learning, and never able to come to the knowledge of the truth. I Tim 3:7* The Bible praises ignorance: *Now when they saw the boldness of Peter and John and perceived that they were unlearned and ignorant men, they marveled; and they took knowledge of them, that they had been with Jesus. Acts 4:13* The Bible proposes a lack of preparation for followers: *...being brought before kings and rulers... Settle it therefore in your hearts, not to meditate before what ye shall answer... Lk 21:12,14* The Bible promotes a child-like understanding: *...Except ye be converted and become as little children, ye shall not enter into the kingdom of heaven. Mt 18:3* The Bible proposes a child-like understanding as praiseworthy...*Jesus said, Let the children come to me...for of such is the kingdom of heaven. Mt 19:14* The Bible proposes a child-like understanding as acceptable...*have ye never read, Out of the mouths of babes and sucklings thou hast perfected praise? Mt 21:16*

Beyond attacking studying, Jesus directly attacks the "learned": *And he said, Woe unto you also, ye lawyers! For ye lade men with burdens grievous to be borne, and ye yourselves touch not the burdens with one of your fingers. Lk 11:46 Then certain of the scribes and Pharisees answered, saying, Master, ... He said to them in reply,... The men of Nineveh shall rise in judgment with this generation and shall condemn it: because they repented ... and a greater than [Jonah] is here. Mt 12:38,39, 41* Jesus follows with scribes and Pharisees described as "the children of hell" (Mt 23:15). *Then came his disciples, and said unto him, Knowest thou that the Pharisees were offended...? But he answered and said... they be blind leaders of the blind. And if the blind lead the blind, both shall fall into the ditch. Mt 15:12,14*

And Jesus went unto the Mount of Olives. And early in the morning, he came again into the temple, and all the people came unto him, and he sat down and taught them. And the scribes and Pharisees... The Pharisees, therefore, said unto him... Then said the Jews... Jesus said unto them... Ye are of your father, the devil, and the lusts of your father ye will do. He was a murderer... and abode not in the truth... he is a liar... and ye do dishonor me... Jn 8

...as he was teaching... Pharisees and doctors of the law... were all amazed... and were filled with fear, saying, We have seen strange things today. Lk 5:17,26 Then Jesus said unto them, Take heed and beware of the leaven of the Pharisees and the Sadducees. Mt 16:6

In another place, Jesus references Pharisees and scribes saying they enlarge the borders of their garments [ostentatiously] (Mt 23:5).

The point is that this sets up followers' acquiescent and ignorant derision of scholarship, leading ever onward to violence. When seeking the original biblical intent for removing authority from those who study devotedly to show themselves approved (2 Tim 2:15), consider temple scholars like Jacob (James) and the brothers of Jesus who had dedicated years to reviewing scripture. Ask who was asking to remove such authority. Jacob, Jesus' brother in the lineage of David, known as `Jacob the Just,` led the Church at Jerusalem, teaching his disciples from Jerusalem's notable position as the geographic center of three continents. Jacob, firmly ensconced at the temple, the banking center of Israel, had assuredly learned multiple languages.

Regarding the lifelong study to which Jacob would have devoted himself, Paul wrote, *"neither give heed to fables and endless genealogies which minister questions rather than [faith]: so do." I Tim 1:4* Rome, incidentally or purposefully supporting Paul's position, confiscated the 'fables' and burned the endless genealogies and debt records stored at the temple. Paul instead honored the freely available gift of "tongues" (I Cor 14:8,23), which require no study, proposing that Israel had "stumbled" in seeking righteousness through the works of the law (Ro 9:31-33).

Note: When the temple fell, and soldiers made off with its profits, the value of gold plummeted (Understanding the Bible, Ray Shortell 2013). Rome tore apart the temple leaving no stone unturned (Mt 24:2 prophesy). The ceiling, made of gold, melted, running between the stones while the temple burned.

Jesus' words echoing through the ages justified those who banished the Jews from Jerusalem while deriding the educated: *Woe unto you scribes and Pharisees, hypocrites! For ye are like unto whited sepulchers which... are... full of dead men's bones... ye are full of hypocrisy and uncleanness... and iniquity... Ye serpents, ye generation of vipers.... ye are the children of them which killed the prophets... some of them [prophets, wise men and scribes] ye shall crucify... Upon you may come all the righteous blood of the earth from Abel to Zecharias... Mt 23:29-35*

Rome continues to aim its derision against education from even before killing the "G-dless heathen" (Gal 2:9), using these words to justify pursuing even more than academics without accountability for the Roman authors who created this context. The Bible cautions against the studious, bookworms, teachers, lawyers, education generally, and most especially the Jewish leadership in Jerusalem <noted above>. And, horror of horrors for those of the scientific method, Christians destroyed alternative documentation, Acts 19:19 recording the first Christian book burning. The derision, coming to fruition in the first century, destroyed the temple, which was torn down stone by stone, with millions of Jews around the Mediterranean killed or conscripted into slavery. Continuing to the present day, the destruction of documentation from alternate viewpoints has kept from us much, from the persecution of science (Galileo) to the promotion of ignorance (Lk 21:12-14 as noted above). Regarding Paul's repudiation of the temple and Jacob's (James') authority, when questioning whether Paul handled himself honestly, one might consider Paul's own words in *II Cor 10:23: All things are lawful for me, but not all things are expedient.* Would Paul call his own holding of the temple authority in derision "edifying"?

Perhaps the Middle Ages ended with the Enlightenment using the Church's metaphor: Jesus was the first to propose that no one sticks a candle under a basket (Mt 5:15) and discussed Christians as filled with light (Mt 6:22-23). Currently, Catholics believe that no one should study the Bible except under the guidance of a priest and in community. This belief stems from the idea that the Church wrote the Bible and continues to do so. Formerly, the Church taught that laity (non-priests) should not learn to read as this kept the people's minds off the thoughts of G-d. Later, the Church condemned private Bibles. Only the rich could afford a book before the dawn of the printing press in the 1500s. The Church felt that anyone owning a Bible should donate it to a church to allow a church somewhere to have access to its writings (Fr. Mike, St. Michael's Woodstock GA ~2005). And there are no Bibles in the pews of Roman Catholic churches, although most

Protestant churches do have Bibles in each row. Although we've mostly eliminated "the Dark Ages" due to its hubris in underestimating our ancestors, a quick review of multitudinous enlightenment sources in art, plays, symphonies, and philosophical treatises such as Thomas Paine's "The Age of Reason" explains why those praising light might have presupposed a dark age.

http://www.catholic.com/magazine/articles/should-catholics-go-to-non-denominational-bible-studies.

6 SACRIFICE: HUMAN, TEMPLE, JESUS, NONE

In the days of Jesus at the dawn of our era, the temple mediated Israel's relationship with our creator with the daily temple sacrifice. Some might wonder at the innocent blood of animals poured forth like a river on the temple mountain (Heb 10:11, II Kings 16:15, Is 1:11, Lev 4:18, Ex 7:20). Priests daily performed the sacrifice, burned some portion, and ate the rest (Num 28:24, Lev 6:16). Regarding sacrifice in Israel, the hidden key is that occasionally it was human sacrifice: ie. Jephthah's daughter as a promised thanksgiving sacrifice (Judges 11:30-39), a Levite to protest a gang rape in Benjamin (Judges 19:29), and nearly so in Abraham's case regarding Isaac (Gen 22:2). Molek and Baal were two local deities who required human sacrifice with whom Israelites occasionally intermarried (Jer 19:2-6, Ps 106:38), much like Moses married the daughter of a Midianite priest (Num 6:29). Israel's Passover in Egypt meant the blood of lambs over the doorposts caused the angel of death to pass by all firstborn (Ex 12:21-23). G-d, therefore, claimed as his right the firstborn of Israel ever since (Ex 13:2). Incidentally, G-d nearly killed Moses until Moses' wife sacrificed her sons' foreskins in his place. She exclaimed, "*...Surely a bloody husband thou art to me*" *Ex 4:25-26,* surely referencing the temple's river of blood pouring forth daily into the ground. Isn't it odd that Moses had not circumcised his children per Gen 17:10? However, back to more generic sacrifice which Jeremiah claims was not commanded until Sinai (Jer 7:22): G-d provided Adam with skins for a covering (Gen 3:21), and Abel sacrificed a lamb (Gen 4:4). At the same time, Cain's grain offering was rejected (Gen 4:3). Noah gave a thanksgiving sacrifice of doves getting a rainbow from G-d in return (Gen 8:20, 9:13). And on it went from there.

The book of Hebrews has some interesting things to say about sacrifice. Abraham nearly sacrificed his son Isaac, for which Heb 11:19 proposes Abraham's belief that G-d could raise Isaac from the dead to fulfill the earlier promise that through Isaac, Abraham would bless the whole world with descendants as numerous as stars (Gen 17:19, 15:5). Christians believe Abraham's near-sacrifice foreshadowed the new covenant when G-d's son was crucified (Lk 20:37) since per the book of Hebrews the blood of bulls and goats was not sufficient to take away sin (Heb 10:4). Incidentally, you'll note ancient temple priests requiring confession of sins along with the offering (Lev 5:5). Christians believe the daily sacrifice stopped because the sacrifice of Jesus was final (Heb 10:10). Some Zealots (Sadducees) felt otherwise – upon the destruction of the temple and removal of the daily sacrifice (Dan 8:11), some including Jacob (James) were said to have become (remained) vegetarian and celibate (1) (Acts 23:12 & 14 recount where zealots planned to neither eat nor drink until after killing Paul who it is presumed had polluted the temple with Greeks or Herodians). As Paul recounts Jacob, possibly minimizing Jacob's abstention: *Refrain from meat offered to idols, fornication, things strangled, and blood. Acts 15:20, 29, 21:25* <note below>

Rather than focus on sacrifice, Jesus focused on something else: Mt 9:13 recounts *Hosea 6:6: For I desired mercy, and not sacrifice; and the knowledge of G-d more than burnt offerings.* As Micah 6:8 puts it: *...what doth the Lord require of thee, but to do justly, and to love mercy, and to walk humbly with thy G-d?* The Bible promotes nothing standing between our Lord and us: *Romans 8:35, 38, 39 – Who shall separate us from the love of Christ? Shall tribulation, or distress, or persecution, or famine, or nakedness, or peril, or sword? ... For I am persuaded, that neither death, nor life, nor angels, nor principalities, nor powers, nor things present, nor things to come, Nor height, nor depth, nor any other creature, shall be able to separate us from the love of G-d, which is in Christ Jesus our Lord.* The Bible promotes nothing as standing between our Lord and us: *Ps 86: 13 – For great is thy mercy towards me: and thou hast delivered my soul from the lowest hell.* The Bible promotes nothing as standing between our Lord and us: *Ps 139:7-8 – Where can I go from your Spirit? Where can I flee from your presence? If I go up to the heavens, you are there; If I make my bed in the depths, you are there.* John, ever the esoteric, recalls Jesus saying: *And I, if I be lifted up from the earth, will draw all men unto me. Jn 12:32*

A question of belief: If Hebrews notes the failure of animal sacrifice to repair a broken relationship with our creator (Heb 10:4), do you believe G-d implemented such sacrifice to foreshadow the sacrifice of

Jesus (Heb 10:10)? Do you believe that forgiveness requires blood (Eph 1:7, Col 1:14)? Do you believe Ps 40:6 that sacrifice is neither desired nor required? Do you believe Jesus' words that learning about the son has replaced the daily blood sacrifice at the Jerusalem temple (Mt 11:29)? For those who have guilt and need for validation or penance ingrained in their souls, might I offer some solace from *Lev 19:18 ...thou shalt love thy neighbor as thyself...* (love thyself). Would you participate in a religion actively sacrificing people (Molek Jer 19:2-6, Baal Ps 106:38, Aztecs of Mexico)? Do you find preferable a religion requiring one human's sacrifice 2000 years ago, as foreshadowed in ancient texts and unabashedly carried out to demonstrate Benjamin's evil (Judges 19:29) or Jephtha's joy (Judges 11:30-39)?

Note: Some find Jacob's (James') request to refrain from blood to go against the Church's drinking of wine as the blood of Christ. However, the gospels have Jesus tying himself directly into the prophecy of being the vine of Judah, the branch of Jesse (David's dad, Is 11:1), and washed in "the blood of grapes" (Gen 49:11), as ascribed to the prophet riding into Jerusalem on an ass and the foal of an ass (Gen 49:10, Mt 21:5).

7 SIN

Augustine's original sin is foundational for Catholicism. However, Adam did not die on the day he ate the fruit (Gen 2:17) unless one counts a thousand years as a day (Ps 90:4, 2 Peter 2:8). I wonder how G-d explained the word "death" to Adam if it failed to exist previously. The biblical principle is that sin separates us from G-d. For instance, in the story of Adam and Eve, we find the two hiding from G-d, who asks: Who told you you were naked (Gen 3:11) as if G-d didn't know? G-d then kicks us out of the garden and sets a flaming sword to prevent our return (Gen 3:24 - Adam in Hebrew also meaning "man"). In Isaiah 59:2, G-d "hides his face" from sinners, and per Micah 3:4, "will not listen". Ps 104:29 notes G-d as taking away the breath, Ps 69:28 as blotting sinners from the book of the living and Rev 3:5 from the book of life. There is a way that seems right to people, says Prov 14:12, but its end is death. Evildoers are cut down like grass (Ps 37:2) and visited to the third and fourth generation (Ex 20:5). G-d threatens to tear sinners in pieces (Ps 50:22), claiming "vengeance is mine" (Ro 12:19, Heb 10:30), a vengeance of eternal fire (Jude 1:7). Depart from evil says Ps 37:27, do good and dwell forevermore. And Isaiah notes pardon and mercy after forsaking evil (Is 55:7).

George Carlin comments on this: Is this the mark of a loving G-d? Wouldn't an omniscient G-d have known the fruit would be eaten? That death would be inevitable? The Bible might be said to have an answer for George. Romans 3:5 asks: Is G-d unrighteous who takes vengeance? In the story of Jonah (ch 4), we find Jonah mourning the death of a gourd plant. G-d relates a concern not only for the gourd, which G-d created for the purpose but for all of humanity, sending Jonah into Nineveh to preach the gospel of repentance.

Paul notes the wages of sin as death (Ro 6:23), which makes only a general sense considering what happens in the bad parts of town. Paul also says that all fall short of the glory of G-d (Ro 3:23). For a general overview of sin at the time of Jesus, the daily temple work (open the gates, burn a few candles, bake some bread, bleed out and eat several cows and doves, and bread & grain Eze 42:18) was thought to restore Israel's relationship with our creator who resided in the inaccessible Holy of Holies. In the time of Jesus, the temple called everyone to a daily remembrance of sin, as does our Lord's prayer (Lk 11:2-4).

John defines sin as transgression of the law (1 Jn 3:3). Elvin Frame (my old Bible study teacher) defined sin as a willful transgression of a known law of G-d. Jacob (James) continues that breaking the smallest of the commandments makes one a debtor to the whole law (Ja 2:10) and goes further by explaining that those who know to do good and yet fail to do so have sinned (Ja 4:17). Jesus explains that his follower's righteousness must exceed that of the scribes and Pharisees (Mt 5:20). Per Paul, the context of the law brings sin into its power, wreaking all manner of havoc upon one's conscience (Ro 7:8), due to sin being unrecognized before being defined by the law (Ro 7:9, I Jn 3:4). Paul claims he was "alive" before receiving the law (Ro 7:9) while later proposing for others that we were dead in our sins before receiving Christ (Eph 2:1) (?!). Per Paul, by defining sin, "the letter of the law" brings "death" (Ro 7:6,10).

Therefore, the question is, there a law outside of "the law"? Paul notes those outside the law as wracking their consciences (Ro 2:15), and regardless of learning the Bible, becoming a law unto themselves (Ro 2:14). Jesus, it might be said, derides these "traditions of men." (Mk 7:8).

Meanwhile, Paul begins discussing "natural law" when talking about the self-imposed shame of men having long hair or praying in a hat (I Cor 11:14, 4), although doubling back on himself to say the church has no custom regarding the issue. Another "law" Paul wishes to impose is that it is good for a man not to marry, which he says is spoken "by permission" (I Cor 7:6). Do these different interpretations reveal a law outside of "The Law"? Hebrews 12:23 proposes that all shall be judged, with Paul noting in Ro 2:12 that those who sin without knowing the law will still die according to the law regardless of having learned the law (not knowing the law being no excuse). Per Jude, the Lord will bring ten thousand angels to convince those living outside of the law of their ung-dly deeds (Jude 1:14-15). Jesus declares an unforgivable sin, blaspheming the Holy Spirit, which preachers propose as learning the truth and remaining outside the fold (Mk 3:29, Lk 12:10). Paul calls willful sin after learning the truth as likewise unforgivable (Heb 10:26).

John, however, softens this hardline on sin, claiming there is a sin "not unto death" (I Jn 5:17) (the Catholic venial sin or minor sin as compared to the mortal sin). Jesus likewise softens "the letter of the law", proposing eating anything, including holy bread on the Sabbath as did David (Mt 12:4) and working on the Sabbath to get your ass out of a pit (Lk 14:5 – yes, it says that). Jesus is apparently also ok with unknowingly walking over unmarked graves (Lk 11:42), although to the best of our knowledge, circumspectly avoiding all of these himself fulfilling each "jot and tittle" (dotting his i(s) and crossing his t(s) - Mt 5:18). For a cross-reference review I Cor 7:8-13, where Paul notes eating offerings to idols as nothing unless you upset a weak believer or are a weak believer yourself... an action which might be sin, depending. Paul continues that for himself, "all is lawful" (I Cor 6:12).

Regarding actual sinners, as reported by Paul, Paul condemned a church-going sinner who was having sex with his mom to be cast out to the judgment of Satan as a bad apple (leaven), which might spoil the whole lot (I Cor 5). Paul repudiated Alexander, the coppersmith, "The Lord reward him according to his works" (II Tim 4:14). In II Tim 4:16, Paul reports: At my first answer, no man stood with me, but all men forsook me: I pray G-d that it may not be laid to their charge. Onesimus might be said to have been a sinner. Onesimus was a runaway enslaved person imprisoned in Rome with Paul. After Onesimus' conversion, Paul returned Onesimus to Philemon, offering to pay for Onesimus' service to Paul during his absence from Philemon (Philemon) <note below>. Regarding Cretians, who were proposing "Jewish fables," Paul reports, "...One of their own said, 'the Cretians are always liars...'. This witness is true." (Titus 12 - 13), suggesting "Their mouths must be stopped." (Tit 1:11)

Does the advent of Jesus create another sin? What would it mean to the law were the new covenant to have generated an additional law? One sin which has enamored Christians since time immemorial is "blaspheming the Holy Spirit" (essentially choosing to remain outside of the church), because Jesus notes this as the sole unforgivable sin (Mk 3:29). John 3:18 notes: ...he that believeth not is condemned... . Or as Jesus said, "If ... they had not witnessed my works, they would not have sin, but now they have rejected my works, me and my Father" (Jn 15:24). Jesus proposes that such have refused the truth due to not wanting light thrown on deeds of darkness (Jn 3:19-20), noting "he who is not with me is against me" (Lk 11:23). Paul chimes in that after learning of Jesus, further sin remains unforgiven (Heb 10:26).

Jesus claims to be non-judgmental (Jn 12:47 If any man hears my words, and believe not, I judge him not: for I came not to judge the world, but to save the world). However, Jesus cries again and again, "Woe unto you, scribes and Pharisees (Mt 23:13)", stands against doctors of the law, turns over banker's tables, throws the marketplace out of the temple (Jn 2:13-17), notes cities condemned to hell for their disbelief (Lk 10:13-15) and teaches disciples to shake the dust from our shoes while walking away from places which do not accept the kingdom (Mt 10:14). Regarding Judas, Jesus' non-judgmental acceptance goes like this: It were good for him were he never born (Mk 14:21). For unfruitful fig-trees, Jesus' judgment is "let no fruit grow on thee henceforward for ever" (Mt 21:19). Similarly, for Samaritans: It is not meet to take the children's bread and cast it to dogs (Mt 15:26) <note below>. And yet, regarding Peter's failings, Jesus' says, "When you have returned. strengthen your brothers." (Lk 22:32) and "Feed my sheep." (Jn 21:16)

Note: Philemon would have been read carefully during the Civil War (War of the Rebellion) between 1862 and 1865 in America. Some argued that following this model, we should have paid enslavers rather than eliminating rightful "property" with a pen. Others argue that the Civil War was about State's rights and not about Slavery. Living in the South for more than two decades, I can testify that both opinions can and do come from the same people. If you're arguing that the US should have redeemed enslaved people, then you're admitting the war was about slavery.

Note: The temple authority reviled dogs due to their inability to differentiate between clean and unclean meat (Chapter 2 – Christianity: Removing Jewish Authority: Friends, Understanding the Bible Ray Shortell 2011). Likewise, the sin of wearing a garment of linen and wool speaks to the Jewish apprehension of children marrying outside of the faith and the same for the law regarding planting different kinds of crops together (Lev 19:19). Native Americans regularly plant corn, beans, and squash together "three sisters." Corn depletes the soil of nitrogen, which beans replenish, while squash keeps away pests and weeds.

8 HEAVEN

Per Josephus, the temple was a metaphor for heaven: Two-thirds were accessible, representing the land and oceans, while behind the temple curtain existed the third part, inaccessible, like air and sky (Antiquities 3.6.4). Regarding a belief in the actual physical place of heaven, like that to which Elijah was taken in a fiery chariot (2 Kings 2:11), the story of Noah suggests a belief in the waters above (Ps 104:3, Ps 148:4): the floodgates of heaven opened covering the whole earth with floodwaters from both heaven above and springs below (Gen 1:7). Job's heaven includes the stars and Mazzaroth, the twelve astrological animals, or signs (Job 38:32). The tower of Babel, where G-d created the world's languages from a single tongue, again notes a belief in an actual physical heavenly realm above (Gen 11:4, Deu 26:15). The apocryphal book of the Secrets of Enoch 3:1 describes Eden as having the waters of Noah's age stored in heaven (Gen 8:11). The ancients believed in firmaments above holding planets in the seven heavens: Sunday for the Sun, Monday for the Moon, Tuesday for Mars, Wednesday for Mercury, Thursday for Jupiter, Friday for Venus, and Saturday for Saturn, the furthest visible planet, considered the highest heaven. The apocryphal gospel of Barnabas, like Kaballah, Jewish mysticism, describes ten heavens – the seven visible heavenly bodies: Sun, Moon, Mercury, Venus, Mars, Jupiter, Saturn, along with the Mazzaroth, earth, and ineffable unity. In the Greek Scriptures, Paul mentions the third heaven in II Cor 12:2. Is 34:4, Matt 24:29, and Rev 6:13 describe the heavens being rolled up like a scroll or shaken with the stars falling from the sky.

The Hebrew Scriptures include no recognition of the concept of immortality or resurrection. Scripture does not mention resurrection until Daniel, which was backdated (1). Until then, the Jewish belief of heavenly reward was in the continued success of one's descendants - a genetic legacy (2). It was not until Roman times when the idea of the immortality of one's soul was inserted into the scriptures (2). Perhaps until then, only a secret Jewish mystic doctrine of Kabbalah (Qabalah) promoted an Egyptian Astrological concept of reincarnation (3). Psalm 110, cited as a source for the immortality of Jesus, was used by David and Maccabeans intent on justifying their children's non-Levitical priesthood: "You are a priest forever in the order of Melchizedek" (4). In the much earlier Gen 14:18, Melchizedek blesses bread and wine as a priest of the most high for Abraham's men, which order is later apparently decreed "forever" upon the non-Levitical priesthood in Ps 110. Psalm 110, following the practice of expounding upon previous scriptures (5) and defending the rights of a non-Levitical priesthood, was highlighted by Maccabeans circa 167 BCE. The Greek Scriptures reinterpret this "forever" as an indication of eternal life (Heb 7). Similarly, it is Hebrews proposing Abraham's attempted sacrifice of Isaac as relying upon a belief in resurrection to fulfill G-d's previous promise of Isaac's genetic legacy (Heb 11:19). Some might suggest additional references to resurrection from Abraham and Isaac "gathered to their ancestors" (Ex 25:8, 35:29), David's going to his dead son (2 Sa 12:23), Jacob to his son Joseph (Gen 37:35), or Josiah to his fathers (2 Ki 22:20, 2 Chr 34:28). However, scriptures before Daniel are perhaps better translated as discussing in more familiar terms, the place to which all men go. While some suggest Psalm 49 or 69:28 as proposing G-d's power beyond the grave, to me, per various translations, these merely refer to the record (sephirot - book, record) one leaves behind of one's passage through life as epitomized by the record left of David's heroes (2 Sam 23:8-39). And in my opinion, Ezekiel's bones merely foreshadow a metaphorically resurrected Israel (Ez 37). Isaiah 25:8 may only discuss eliminating war and its genocide when such death is swallowed up in victory by the rulership of Isaiah's prophesied world king. Paul again reinterprets Isaiah's blessing upon Israel's descendants as immortal resurrection (I Cor 15:54), which is reinvoked with Revelation concurring with Isaiah that our eternal G-d shall destroy death (Rev 21:4). Reviewing further references to resurrection or eternal life, the assumption into heaven of Enoch (Gen 5:24) and Elijah (2 Kings 2:11) remain unexplained. In the Acts, Jesus also ascends into the clouds (Acts 1:9). And in 1950, in the Apostolic Constitution <Munificentissimus Deus>, Pope Pius XII proclaimed the Assumption of Mary a dogma of the Catholic Church that Mary had been assumed into heaven (https://www.ewtn.com/library/ANSWERS/AOFMARY.HTM). At the transfiguration, both Moses and Elias (Elijah?) speak with Jesus upon the mountain with the limited (limited!) audience of Peter, Jacob (James), and John (Lk 9:29-30). Some suggest that Moses and Elijah or Enoch and Elijah are the two required witnesses (Deu 19:15) who, per Revelation, appear in Jerusalem, die, resurrect, and leave again (Rev 11:3-12). Summing up, Jesus enunciates resurrection while arguing against temple Sadducees, who undoubtedly knew their scriptures, yet gainsaying Daniel, Ezekiel, Isaac, David, Isaiah, and Ps 49, don't believe in an afterlife (Mt 22:23, 30). Jesus, pulling his best references, contends that because G-d claimed to be the G-d of Abraham, Isaac, and Jacob, that these three patriarchs still live since the claim is in the present tense rather than in the past tense (Mt 22:32). Sadducees would have noted Jacob's remains interred nearby (Gen 50:13). Jesus fails to take the argument further, continuing by saying we will sit down with Abraham, Isaac, and Jacob in heaven (Mt 8:11).

The gospel of John stands outside of time. Written as the last of the gospels, possibly only having heard of, but without access to other gospels, John recognizes that Jesus has not immediately returned (Jn 21:23). John deity is immanent, a creator who takes part in the daily life of the community as per Jn 1:14: *...we beheld his glory...* Jn 11:26: *And whosoever liveth and believeth in me shall never die.* Believers pass from death to life without needing the grave (Jn 5:24-25, 11:26). Per Jn 10:38 *...the Father is in me, and I in him.* 17:26 *And I have declared unto them thy name and will declare it: that the love wherewith thou hast loved me may be in them, and I in them.* Jn 3:27 - *A man can receive nothing except it be given him from heaven.* Jn 6:51 - *I am the bread from heaven* or (Jn 11:25) *I am the resurrection and the life.* However, John references heaven with many mansions, confusingly breaking with the Johannine tradition of Jesus or the Holy Spirit bringing life here and now without the need for future reward (Jn 14:2).

In my opinion, the Bible promotes an evolving promise of paradise, with most earlier scriptures at later authors' disposal (6). Heaven is a place beyond compare: Paul says it has not entered into the heart of man regarding that which is prepared (I Cor 2:9). Jesus notes getting into heaven as challenging as getting a camel through the eye of the needle (from the Middle Ages, supposedly a steep and winding entrance to the temple but recently debunked; Mk 10:25), like finding a narrow gate while the crowd takes the roadway (Mt 7:14), like a pearl on sale for which merchants would sacrifice everything (Mt 13:46). Five wise virgins, Jesus relates, would wait all night prepared with extra oil for the wedding feast (Mt 16:19). Jesus proposes in Jewish kingly fashion with a touch of Roman resurrection that disciples will eat at his table and sit upon twelve thrones judging the twelve tribes of Israel (Lk 22:30), with Matthew writing in pure Roman fashion (Appendix: Conquering Death) that at Jesus' resurrection the saints of Jerusalem came out of their graves (Mt 27:53). The earlier story of promise, the promised land when Israel was in Egypt, was Canaan where Abraham had previously set an altar (Gen 12,13), a land flowing with milk and honey (Ex 3:8, etc.), which some suggested as already existing in Egypt in captivity (Num 16:13). Isaiah improved this promise suggesting a land flowing with butter and honey (Is 7:22). When Israel possessed Canaan, the promise became a time when every nation would seek the throne of David for judgment (I Kings 2:45, Deu 15:6, Ps 72:11, Is 2:2) while Israel, protected by the eternal G-d (Deu 33:27), who curses those who curse Israel (Gen 12:3, Nu 24:9), who destroyed the nations before Israel (Ps 135:10), who commanded the destruction of the Bashanites (Deu 3:2) and Sihon (Deu 2:32-34), giving inhabited Canaan to Israel (Gen 14:21, Ex 23:23), will return blessings to all nations through Israel (Gen 18:18, Note: this last sentence is indeed irony). Following the ancient promise forward, Ex 9:6 proposes a time when no priests will be required because Israel will be a nation of priests. In the more recent Psalms, we will be G-ds (Ps 82:6, Jn 10:34). The promise is a day when seven women ask to be called by the name of each man (Is 4:1), with Daniel blending the promises of both Roman resurrection and Jewish rulership with an everlasting kingdom (Dan 2:44) to which the nations of the world bring treasure (Rev 21:24).

Another example where biblical authors build upon previous authors regards The Book of Life: There are only two references to this heavenly book outside of Revelation. In my opinion, Psalms 69:28 "mesepher" translates into "being accounted" as among the land of the living (Job 28:13), while the second half of Ps 69:28 compares forgotten evil people against the records of heroes like David's righteous warriors from II Sam 23:39. The second reference to the Book of Life is in the letter of Paul to the Philippians 4:3

and is accurately rendered "book," but is therefore the only reference to the "Book of Life" outside of Revelation, including no further explanation or context. The phrase stands on its own without context in Philippians. In my opinion, the authors/editors of Philippians had a mistranslation of "mesepher" as "book". However, both of our oldest copies of the Bible from the 4th century (Sinaiticus & Vaticanus) list the phrase, copied from originals by different scribes, meaning the word in the Bible purposefully describes the mindset of its Greek authors regarding their interpretation of ancient Hebrew. Meanwhile, Revelation includes references to not only the single Book of Life where you must find your name, but also to libraries of books and records (Rev 20:12).

Jesus uses multiple metaphors to describe heaven. Jesus compares those with the knowledge of heaven to homeowners bringing forth both new and old treasures (Mt 13:52), saying this knowledge of heaven spreads as quickly as leaven (yeast through bread)(Mt 13:35), used as a positive metaphor as opposed to his standard negative context for the leaven of the Pharisees and Sadducees (Mt 16:6). Jesus both ascends to heaven in a cloud (Mk 16:19, Jn 12:32) and explains that the kingdom of G-d is within us (Lk 17:21). To get into heaven, Jesus proposes not sinning and selling all your belongings for the poor (Mt 19:21), loving the Father by following Jesus' commandments (Jn 14:21), and by learning about Jesus (Mt 11:29).

An overview for the rest of this chapter on heaven, as per my belief of heaven as a developing concept, depends upon the order in which authors wrote. First, Paul's actual books make several pronouncements: "To die is gain." Ph 1:21 and being immediately with Jesus (2 Cor 5:6,8). Next come the synoptic gospels Mark, Luke, and Matthew. Today you shall be with me in paradise (Lk 23:43). Heaven is good (Mt 13:45). The Father and angels will reward everyone according to our works (Mt 16:27), where marriage will be as different for us as it is for angels (Mk 12:25). Next are the post-humous writings of Paul: We will reign (2 Tim 2:12) and have eternal life (1 Tim 6:19). Finally, Revelation presents a full-blown heaven with angels and harps (Rev 5:11, 14:2-3) and martyrs around the throne, begging for G-d's judgment on the earth. Scholars attempt to provide a cohesive theology of heaven from this melee of scripture but neglect the multitude of beliefs sponsored by biblical authors, including the Jewish non-belief of, or even finding useless, any discussion of heaven due to, in my opinion, a belief in reincarnation. Scholars also discard stories like Lazarus in heaven unable to grant a rich man's desires (Lk 16:23-25), much like scientists discarding data thought to be a "gross error."

From the oldest to the newest of the heavenly promises:
Job 38:19 "the abode of light"
Ps 103:9 The Lord hath prepared his throne in heaven; and his kingdom ruleth over all.
Is 45:23 ...unto me every knee shall bow, every tongue shall swear.
I Cor 9:25 ...we shall be given an incorruptible crown...
James 2:5 Hearken, my beloved brethren, Hath not G-d chosen the poor of this world rich in faith, and heirs of the kingdom which he hath promised to them that love him?
Ja 1:12 "crown of life"
Mt 25:34 ...Come, ye blessed of my Father, inherit the kingdom prepared for you from the Foundation of the world:
Lk 17:21 ...the kingdom of G-d is within you.
Ph 2:10-11 That at the name of Jesus every knee should bow, of things in heaven and things in earth and things under the earth; And that every tongue should confess that Jesus Christ is Lord, to the glory of G-d the Father.
I Tim 6:19 Laying up in store for themselves a good foundation against the time to come, that they may lay hold on eternal life.
II Tim 4:8 "Henceforth is laid up for me a crown of righteousness..."
I Pet 5:4 We shall be given a crown of glory.

Jn 18:36 My kingdom is not of this world.

Rev 21:4 And G-d shall wipe away all tears from their eyes; and there shall be no more death, neither sorrow nor crying, neither shall there be any more pain: for the former things are passed away

Rev 11:15 The kingdoms of this world are become the kingdoms of our Lord, and of his Christ; and he shall reign for ever and ever.

And, Oh, the judgments!

Ro 14:10-12 But why dost thou judge thy brother? Or why dost thou set at naught thy brother, for we shall all stand before the judgment seat of Christ. For it is written, As I live, saith the Lord, every knee shall bow to me, and every tongue shall confess to G-d. So then every one of us shall give account of himself to G-d.

2 Cor 5:10 For we must all appear before the judgment seat of Christ; that every one may receive the things done in his body, according to that he hath done, whether it be good or bad.

I Cor 3:13-14 Every man's work shall be made manifest: for the day shall declare it because it shall be revealed by fire, and fire shall try every man's work of what sort it is. If any man's work abide which he hath built thereupon, he shall receive a reward.

Mt 24:14 And this gospel of the kingdom shall be preached in all the world for a witness unto nations; And then shall the end come.

Mt 7:23 And then I will profess unto them, I never knew you: depart from me, ye that work iniquity.

2 Tim 2:12 If we suffer, we shall also reign with him: If we deny him, he shall also deny us.

And Revelation finally attempts to explain everything:

Rev 20:3 - The dragon is cast into the bottomless pit for a thousand years, before being loosed again for a little season (gotta love those bottomless pits) (gotta love dragons crawling out of bottomless pits).

I believe Revelation was included in the canon because other books failed to include further information on heaven. Until Revelation, Paul and the gospels offer a mere heaven for believers against the judgment of hell. Revelation increases the stakes by relating details of an eternal judgment, which apparently has yet to happen, where you first find your name in the Book of Life (Rev 20:15) and afterward have a judgment regarding how large your crown should be. Whether or not you have passed through the guarded but open twelve gates made of pearl to find your name remains undefined (Rev 21). Heavenly martyrs surround G-d's throne, praying the Lord to deliver justice quickly by pouring his cup of wrath upon all the earth.

Revelation brings to mind those who have gotten victory over the beast (Rev 15:2), are praised as good and faithful servants (Mt 25:21), and are written into the book of life (Rev 21:27) where we get new names (Rev 2:17), shine like the sun (Mt 13:43) or stars (Ph 2:5), are clothed in white (Rev 3:5), playing harps while worshiping around the throne (Rev 15:2), eating month by month from the twelve fruits of the tree of life in paradise (Rev 2:8), holding palm branches and shepherded by the lamb to living fountains of waters (Rev 7:17), where the water of life flows as a river proceeding from the throne (Rev 22:1), the throne of our Father (Mt 23:22), surrounded by four living creatures full of eyes front and back (Rev 4:6), with the seven spirits of G-d (Rev 4:5), a place where the will of our Father is done (Lk 11:2), shining like the sun (Rev 3), the new Jerusalem with streets of transparent gold (Rev 21:21).

At the first judgment, angels will reap the earth (Rev 14:7) and separate the wheat from the weeds (Mt 13:38-42), gathering the elect from the ends of heaven and earth (Mk 13:27). The prepared shall get in (five wise virgins Mt 25:1-13), along with 144,000 of the twelve tribes (12,000 from each, Rev 7:4, 14:1), everyone finding their names in the Book of Life <above>. There may be only one Judgment as in Lk 19:11-27 praising the good servants and setting the best over much. Or perhaps there are seven harvests (reference Elvin Frame, my old Bible Study teacher from the Church of the Nazarene in Marietta, GA, circa 1994). 1) The first fruits - Jesus (I Cor 15:20). 2) The saints who arose at his resurrection (Mt 27:52). 3) Opening of graves and sea at his return (I Th 4:13-17, Rev 20:13). 4-6) Us caught up in the clouds (I Thes 4:17) through the tribulation. 7) the last gleanings (those who wavered, were lost, and yet survive the tribulation remaining, in the end, faithful, Rev 9:4, 11:13). The second judgment may give crowns of glory to the good and faithful servants (Mt 25:23, Ro 8:18, I Cor 9:25, II Tim 4:8, I Pe 5:4, Ja 1:12).

At the judgment, heaven and earth may become one as in the Lord's prayer: Thy kingdom come, thy will be done on earth as it is in heaven (Mt 6:10). In Mt 28:18, Jesus declares that all power has been given to himself. Ps 37:11 notes the meek inheriting the earth, which Jesus quotes in Mt 5:5. Heb 1:10 further explains that the Lord created the earth. The earth is the Lord's, declares I Cor 10:26. Heb 6:7 says the Lord blesses the earth with rain. Heb 12:26-27 notes the future shaking of the heavens and earth so that that which is unshakable may remain. Heb 8:13 indicates even the old covenant passing away. Jesus notes the earth's possible passing: Heaven and earth shall pass away, but my words shall not (Mt 24:35).

Or perhaps there is a new heaven and a new earth as proposed by Is 65:17 and II Peter 3:13 with a new Jerusalem in Rev 3:12, the heavenly city Heb 11:13. Paul notes the Jerusalem above (a heavenly or spiritual Jerusalem) in Gal 4:26, saying that we shall all be changed (I Cor 14:51). We shall all have new incorruptible bodies (I Cor 15:51-53), glorious bodies (Ph 3:20), clothing our spirits with our house from heaven (2 Cor 5), as opposed to [per above - 2 Pt 3:7] Peter's destruction of the earth and heaven by fire.

Heaven will be our place of eternal life through Christ Jesus (Mt 25:46), yes, life after death (Jn 11:25), a place where everything will be known (Mt 10:26-27), a place where our eternal crown awaits (I Cor 9:25) for when Jesus returns (Acts 9:11) in clouds of glory (Mt 26:64) like lightning flashing from one side of the heaven to the other (Mt 24:27) because we are cared for more even than sparrows which falling from the sky do not go unnoticed (Mt 10:29-31), prepared for glory (Is 43:6-7), by the good works we have done (Phil 4:1), for people we have saved (II Tim 4:8), for having run the good race (I Cor 9:13), for having saved the lost sheep by returning repentant sinners to the fold (Lk 15:4-7), for visiting widows and the fatherless (Ja 1:27), and prisoners (Mt 25:36, 45).

Suggested reading: Chapters one and two of Genesis followed by chapters twenty and twenty-one of Revelation (first and last two chapters of the Bible).

And no chapter on heaven would be complete without a discussion of angels:

The Bible only lists three of the four arch-angels of Jewish lore: Michael the warrior (Dan 10:13, Jude 1:9, Rev 12:7), Raphael the healer (Sirach), and Gabriel the herald (Dan 8:16, 9:21, Lk 1:19, 26) with Uriel, the angel of fate excluded from scripture (Fr Mike of St. Michael's circa 2006). Jacob wrestles with an angel (Gen 32) and dreams of angels ascending and descending from heaven upon a ladder (Gen 28:2). Daniel 10:13 has an angel restrained by another for twenty-one days until Michael assists. Israel is led by an angel when escaping Egypt while the Lord appears as a cloud in the day and pillar of fire in the night (Ex 14:9). Cherubim, winged protectors, are also in heaven (Ex 37:9). Jesus says his return will be with angels in the clouds, where marriage will be as different for us as it is for angels (Mk 12:25), when we will see heaven will opened and angels ascending and descending upon the Son of man (Jn 1:51) with the Father and angels who will reward everyone according to our works (Mt 16:27). Rev 12:1-9 describes Michael in heaven leading the angels who cast out Satan and his angels down to the earth. Heb 12:11 notes the saints around us now like a cloud, while Elisha prayed for the eyes of some to be opened to the heavenly host apparently always present (2 Kings 6:18-15).

Peter's Keys

Do Peter's keys jingle? If the kingdom is within, will they tingle?

What could there be to bind in Heaven? Should we fear there might yet be leaven*?

These gates of heaven and gates of hell, so many gates** it's tough to tell.

If angels separate the wheat from the tares***, this Book of Life judgment**** will happen wheres?

This king of heaven upon his throne: Did he lock the door to the place we call home?

And there's the limit of the sea, where G-d claims the bars have been set,

And yet, and yet, and yet, the oceans rise, neglecting the words on the page.

A new earth, ours destroyed and shaken, must we go? Will all be taken?

How then shall the meek inherit the earth?

And if both old and new earths remain per the Bible, which is which, and are those who teach wrongly liable?

Mt 16:19 - Jesus will give Peter "the keys to the kingdom of heaven: and whatsoever you bind on earth shall be bound in heaven, and whatever you loose on earth shall be loosed in heaven."

- * Leaven – Yeast; ...beware of the leaven of the Pharisees and of the Sadducees... (Mt 16:1-12) It is like leaven, which a woman took and hid in three measures of meal, till the whole was leavened (Lk 13:21).
- **Gate of heaven Gen 28:17, Gates of pearl Rev 21:21, Gates of death Job 38:17, Gates of hell (Mt 16:18), Doors of the shadow of death Job 38:17, Windows of heaven Gen 7:11, Fountains of the deep...stopped Gen 7:11, Land of the shadow of death Is 9:2, Valley of the shadow of death Ps 23:4
- ***Angels separate the wheat from the tares - Mt 13:37-43
- ****Book of Life - Rev 20:12
- New heaven and new earth; the first passed away - Rev 21:1 The meek shall inherit the earth Mt 5:5

Or who shut up the sea with doors, when it brake forth as if it had issued out of the womb? When I made the cloud the garment thereof, and thick darkness a swaddling band for it, And brake up for it my decreed place, and set bars and doors, And said, Hitherto shalt thou come, but no further: and here shall thy proud waves be stayed? Job 38:8-11

...In the days of the Son of man. ... Two men shall be in the field; the one shall be taken, and the other left. And they answered and said unto him, Where, Lord? And he said unto them, Wheresoever the body is, [carcass Mt 24:28] thither will the eagles be gathered together. Lk17:26, 36, 37

Note: I've tested this, acting like a wounded rabbit crawling across a hill. The eagle came within 20 feet, scaring the dickens out of me. Since believers are to be taken (I Thes 4:13-18), and the rest remain (Rev 9:4), my interpretation is that Jesus said that believers' carcasses would remain behind, although most interpret differently.

Notes:
Original writings of Paul - Romans, I & II Corinthians, Galatians, Philippians, I Thessalonians & Philemon.
Secondary writings of Paul - I & II Timothy, Titus, II Thessalonians, Ephesians, Colossians
Pg 93, Forged! Bart D Ehrman 2011

9 HELL

Are you aware that many Jewish people are reincarnationists (1) and that many rabbis believe that all Jewish people were present at Mt. Sinai when Moses delivered the Ten Commandments (2)? With reincarnation in mind, what then would a Jewish person believe about hell? Mind you, Paul likewise dealt with people who felt that grace permitted shenanigans (Ro 6:1). My understanding of the Jewish belief is that Satan was originally G-d's prosecuting attorney, viewed as a servant of the most high accusing all, as Satan did to Job (Job 1).

Luke's story of Lazarus creates a problem for many Christian authors who note a lack of support for its description of death elsewhere in the Bible: There was a certain rich man... and in hell he lifted his eyes, being in torments, ... and he cried and said.. have mercy on me... for this flame torments me. But [Abraham] said... between you and us there is a great gulf fixed: so that they which would pass from hence to you cannot; neither can they pass to us, that would come from thence (Lk 16:23). Is this a version of hell where consciousness exists? Lazarus' hell is a place of thirst and torment as opposed to the fiery hell of I Pet 4:12, Heb 10:27. Can one reason from hell? Can one communicate with other souls while in hell? Are souls with Abraham in communication with souls in hell? Are souls with Abraham in heaven? Or is this merely a metaphoric discussion from Jesus, a warning to avoid the pains of hell (Ps 116:3)?

Another verse speaks of the Father having made everything (Jn 1:3). Did the Father create hell? Was hell a part of creation? Can the Holy Spirit reach into the depths of hell? One verse says: If I ascend up into heaven, thou art there: if I make my bed in hell, behold, thou art there (Ps 139:8). Jonah reports calling to the Lord from hell: ...out of the belly of hell cried I and thou heardest my voice (Jonah 2:2). The book of Jonah also highlights a tall plant dying, which angered Jonah as having been pre-destined to its fate (Jonah 4). A famous verse, Mt 16:18, refers to "the gates of hell" as not prevailing against the church. Would you consider this battle odd since G-d commands Satan (Job 1:12), created hell (Jn 1:3), and presumably its gates? Job 26:6 notes that hell is naked before him, and destruction hath no covering. In the book of Jude 1:9, archangel Michael contends with the devil over Moses' body, and in Revelation 12:7, St. John the Divine records that the Dragon, the serpent (Eve's?), Satan, and the Devil are the same (Rev 20:2).

The Catholic Church has an intriguing relationship with hell and a limbo place called purgatory (3). More noticeably, Protestants neglect purgatory, preaching only about the dangers of hell. One might say that Protestant ministers use fire and brimstone as a theological arsenal (4). Recently, the Catholic Church has attempted to moderate this view of hell. Purgatory no longer exists per the Catholic Church, much like the Dark Ages (Both have been done away with. Stay posted for further updates from the Pope. The Church pardoned Galileo in 1992, and in preparation for the 2000 year of jubilee, Pope John Paul promulgated Pius XII's 1946 bishops' consultation and resulting 1950 infallible declaration of the divinely revealed dogma of Mary's assumption http://www.ncregister.com/blog/jimmy-akin/the-assumption-of-mary-12-things-to-know-and-share2). The Pope has further said that hell is only a state of mind (5), which church theologians have since feverishly attempted to reinterpret/mitigate (http://www.ovrlnd.com/Cults/poprejectshell.html).

Hell and destruction are before the Lord says Prov 15:11. Another reference from Jesus regarding hell says: And fear not them which kill the body, but are not able to kill the soul: but rather fear him which is able to destroy both body and soul in hell (Mt 10:28) or him who has power to cast you into hell (Lk 12:5). However, St. John the divine tells that hell itself will be destroyed in a lake of fire: ...and death and hell delivered up the dead which were in them: and they were judged every man according to their works. And death and hell were cast into the lake of fire. This is the second death (Rev 20:14), which 2 Pet 2:4 supports, where everyone returns from hell to judgment, including angels, before the earth and heavens suffer fiery destruction (2 Pet 3:7) and death and hell get destroyed (Rev 20:14). Hell is therefore temporary although presumably not the damnation of hell (Mt 23:33) and eternal fire (Ja 3:6, Mark 9:45).

Here's an earlier and more peaceful version of hell from an angry prophet prior to Mark's eternal damnation (3:29):

...the mighty that are fallen of the uncircumcised, which are gone down to hell with their weapons of war: and they have laid their swords under their heads, but their iniquities shall be upon their bones, though they were the terror of the mighty in the land of the living. Ez 32:27

Or perhaps there is a second judgment with a second death where death gets destroyed (Rev 20:14 - a second death only mentioned in Revelation). And Paul noted G-d as having prepared some for destruction to show his glory as when he hardened the heart of Pharaoh to inflict the ten plagues on Egypt (Ro 9:17-22), as G-d did for Jonah's gourd tree (Jonah 4:6-10), and Jesus did for a fig tree. Note: The Bible neglects Jesus' creation of the fig tree, Mt 21:9, although "through him, all things were made" per the Apostolic Creed.

10 TAXES

For Israel, in the first century, taxes meant acquiescence to Rome. Paul's viewpoint is seemingly direct: Pay your taxes (Ro 13:13). Paul's seemingly straightforward tax stance, therefore, contended with a larger group of zealots around the temple. Jacob (James) lived in Jerusalem celibate, prayerful, vegetarian, of the lineage of David from the house of Judah, and yet still apparently a priest who visited the Holy of Holies at least once (pg 310, James, the Brother of Jesus, Robert Eisenman 1997). In my opinion, Jacob shared a direct link with the Essenes. In my opinion, the Essenes lived in peace with an absence of money, believing that Roman money, with its rendering of Caesar was in direct violation of the second commandment regarding graven images (Ex 20:4, Deu 5:8). Additionally, the Essenes and Zealots would not have accepted Roman coinage due to rules about not allowing a king who is not a brother - not Jewish (Deu 17:15).

The potential conflict between Roman taxation and Essenic beliefs displayed by Jacob's vegetarianism and the Essene reticence around money would have distressed everyone seeking peace. For example, how would Rome have taxed the twelve? Rome might have seized the money holder, Judas (Jn 13:10), found very little for thirteen men and demanded the leader.

Like John the Baptist, Jacob (James) was "Poor" and lived in the wilderness. John ate locusts and wild honey. How would Rome have viewed this? How would Rome have collected taxes from John's followers? John, per the Bible, was killed for noting Herod should not marry his brother's wife. The Bible fails to note Herodias as Herod's and Phillip's half-sister or Herod's divorce from the daughter of King Areatas with whom Paul quarreled (Acts 9:25, II Cor 11:33). Do you suppose John's prison stay may have been while Rome ascertained John's ability to pay a fine? (Acts 24:26 notes Felix hoping for a bribe to let Paul go free.) Are you aware that a "poll" tax originally took its meaning from "head", where people would trim hair (Eze 44:23 KJV/AMP biblegateway.com – poll/hair)? Now Paul paid the "poll" tax, in his words at the insistence of Jacob (James) (Acts 21:24). Perhaps taking John's head was symbolic of what happens to people who fail to pay the tax/bribe (Mk 6:24).

With no evidence to substantiate, I believe Rome would have been happy to have taken livestock as payment. However, vegetarians such as Jacob and the Essenes would have had nothing to give Rome. Some Essenes believed that killing any animal would no longer be forgiven after the temple's destruction, and holy sacrifice no longer available (p293 James, the Brother of Jesus, Robert Eisenman 1997). Thus, vegetarianism generally means no livestock. Perhaps this timing is off since Jacob was a life-long vegetarian before Rome destroyed the temple, like his father who supposedly lived to 120 (pg 340 James, the Brother of Jesus, Robert Eisenman 1997). Perhaps the Essenes viewed the temple as already polluted with Rome holding the priestly vestments (Chap 20 Family of Paul – Understanding the Bible – Ray Shortell 2011) and installing whosoever they wished (pg 182 James, the Brother of Jesus, Ray Shortell 1997).

At Jesus' trial, one of the accusations was that he told people not to pay the tax (Mt 17:24, Lk 23:2). In the gospels, Jesus renders a mixed message regarding what belongs to the temple and what belongs to Rome, "Render unto Caesar what is Caesar's and unto G-d what is G-d's," as if the Roman emperor were outside of Paul's "natural law" and not created by our creator, although the gospels having been written by all accounts after the writings of Paul. And yet Jesus fails to touch the money paid to the temple, the "temple tax," as if some ancient Levitical law commanded such a tax. There is a mystery surrounding who this head tax collector might have been (Hint: It was Herod p109 James, the Brother of Jesus, Robert Eisenman 1997), and we wonder where in Rome's power scheme tax collectors like Matthew and Zacchaeus might have fallen (Mt 10:3, Lk 19:2).

11 DEATH OF JACOB (JAMES)

Hegesippus in his Memoirs - "The aforesaid Scribes and Pharisees, accordingly, placed Jacob upon a wing of the Temple, and cried out to him 'O thou Just One, whom we ought all to credit, since the people are led astray after Jesus that was crucified, declare to us what is the door to Jesus that was crucified.' But he answered with a loud voice, 'Why do you ask me regarding Jesus the Son of Man? He is now sitting in the heavens on the right hand of Great Power, and is about to come on the clouds of Heaven.'…

And they began to stone him as he did not die immediately when cast down; but turning round, he knelt down, saying, 'I beseech Thee, O Lord God and Father, forgive them, for they know not what they do.' Thus they were stoning him, when one of the priests of the sons of Rechab, a son of the Rechabites spoken of and by Jeremiah the prophet, cried out, saying, 'Stop! What are you doing? The Just is praying for you.'

Thus one of them, a fuller, beat out the brains of the Just with the club he used to beat out clothes. Thus he suffered martyrdom, and they buried him on the spot where his tombstone still remains, close to the Temple. He became a faithful witness; both to the Jews and to the Greeks that Jesus is the Christ. Immediately after this, Vespasian invaded and took Judea." (Hegesippus as quoted in Eusebius, Ecclesiastical History, Book II, xxiii)

http://www.biblesearchers.com/hebrewchurch/primitive/primitive15.shtml.

12 ATHIESM

My purpose in discussing atheism is to dispel ignorance. Christians regularly impute motivations to atheists, which, by my definition, is ignorance. To not be ignorant when attributing motivation to anyone perceived outside of a group, people referenced in the third person as other or they, use a quotation. Changing the context of a quote is acceptable while changing its meaning is not. (In the past, yellow dog journalists would quote politicians leaving out important modifiers like `not`.)

Regarding whether an atheist can be a moral person, Christians often raise the question "How?" or "Why?" Listening to multiple atheists (Richard Dawkins, George Carlin, Christopher Hitchens), the general response is, "of course atheists have morals". This respectful dialogue between Christians and Atheists is crucial in promoting mutual understanding and respect. Atheists tend to follow-up by reviewing multiple other non-Christian and pre-Christian religions. Some people even question whether Christians have morals (Native Americans; Crusaders). Sadducees (temple zealots), if you believe Mt 22:23, had a pretty solid code of morals even while not believing in resurrection.

APPENDIX: BROTHERS, PEOPLE, TIMELINE

Appendix Brothers
Questions for Christians

1) Why, in your opinion, doesn't every Sunday school class have the names of the twelve apostles memorized? What implications might this have around understanding the apostles and their role in the early church?

The twelve apostles, a crucial aspect of religious studies, do not have a set listing. The various lists in the Bible do not match each other. Additionally, four have duplicates. For instance, there is Jacob (James), the greater, the son of Alphaeus and James the lesser. Per Acts 12:2, Herod killed James, the brother of John, with the sword. Per Josephus, somebody threw Jacob (James) from the temple in 62 and killed him. Peter was named Simon Peter or Simeon, one of the original twelve tribes of Israel. Judas was also known as Judas Thomas or Thomas Didymus, both of which mean "the twin" in different languages. In an apocryphal gospel, Thomas is mistaken for Jesus.

From Matthew 10:
2 Simon, who is called Peter, and Andrew his brother; James the son of Zebedee, and John his brother;
3 Philip, and Bartholomew; Thomas, and Matthew the publican; Jacob (James) the son of Alphaeus, and Lebbaeus, whose surname was Thaddaeus;
4 Simon the Canaanite, and Judas Iscariot, who also betrayed him.

From Luke 14:
14 Simon, (whom he also named Peter,) and Andrew his brother, Jacob (James) and John, Philip, and Bartholomew,
15 Matthew and Thomas, Jacob (James) the son of Alphaeus, and Simon called Zelotes,
16 And Judas, the brother of Jacob (James), and Judas Iscariot, which also was the traitor.

2) Why doesn't every Sunday school class discuss the four brothers of Jesus?

These are known as having eight namesakes among the apostles:
From Matthew 13:55 – *Jacob (James), Joses, Simon, Judas*
From Mark 6:3 – *Jacob (James), Joses, Juda, Simon*

Please consult James, the Brother of Jesus 1993, Dr. Robert Eisenman, for further information.

Appendix People
Sadducees - Temple worship focused. The root word "Tzaddick" or "Zadoc" means "Zealous" as in: ...the zeal of thine house hath eaten me up (Jn 2:17). Sadducees would have loved animal sacrifice and probably carried knives with which to circumcise or kill any who dared discuss theology. Sadducees sought a worthy High Priest.

Pharisees – Synagogue-worship focused. Pharisees were "accommodators" who sought no waves with Rome. Pharisee leadership is known as a Rabbi, teacher, or synagogue official, similar to Catholic priests, who are called "Father". Rabbis consented to Romans taxes, as in: ...Render therefore unto Caesar the things that are Caesar's; and unto G-d the things that are G-ds (Mt 22:21).

The High Priest – Genealogically, priests were to be of the tribe of Levi and the house of Aaron. The

High Priest was a central figure in the temple who passed through the curtain once a year during Yom Kippur. By the time of Jesus, the Maccabees had taken over who were possibly not even Levitical (Chapter 8 – Heaven – Angels – reference 4), and the Roman ruler selected the High Priest from among those generally acceptable and subservient to Rome. Rome controlled the priestly robe in the Roman tower overlooking the temple on the opposing hill (vestments: Chapter 20 – The Family of Paul – Understanding the Bible, Ray Shortell 2011).

Jesus - Born 6-7 CE of a Davidic and Priestly lineage (like Jacob (James)) and crucified circa 40 CE (my opinion).

Jacob (James) - The older brother of Jesus who led the Jerusalem church after the crucifixion and prayed in the Holy of Holies of the temple, to which only the High Priest had access. Jude references himself as the brother of Jacob (James) rather than as the brother of our Lord. Jacob dies in 62 at the age of 96, per Josephus. The name James is a "mistranslation" of Jacob

Paul - Originally named Saul after the king who preceded David. Josephus may have written of Paul under the name Saulos. Saulos visited Jerusalem during the famine of 46 -48. Paul claimed unto himself the title of apostle unto the gentiles (Rom 11:13) and wrangled for authority at the Jerusalem council against James (Gal 2:1-10). Saul had close Roman relatives in more than a few cities.

Stephen - A Greek follower of Christ, this means non-Jewish or Gentile, killed at the hand of Paul (Acts 22:20), who claimed to be the apostle unto the Gentiles (Rom 11:13). Was he the first martyr? Stephen is a Greek Christian before Paul preached to the Gentiles. Stephen preaches to the High Priest on the temple steps, although the Sadducees/Sicarii don't question Stephen regarding whether or not he is circumcised.

Maccabees - The priestly descendants of a Zealous Jew who may or may not have been of the lineage of Levi and house of Aaron. Ps 110 may have been authored by these explaining to their posterity the source of their claim to the temple (Postscript: Failed Messianic Prophesies, Understanding the Bible, Ray Shortell 2011).

The Chief Tax Collector - Herod – Rome referred to Herod as Jewish. However, Sadducees did not accept him as a brother (Deu 17:15). Herod married or killed the Maccabees as referenced in (Mt 2:18). Herod's son, Herod, married a half-sister Herodias after divorcing the daughter of king Areatas of Damascus from across the Jordan. Herod had John killed to prevent an uprising per Josephus, after which the Jews blamed Herod's battle losses on being unworthy - Herod's Idumeans switched sides in the battle. Josephus notes the Idumeans eventually taking pity on Herod and returning as his foremost supporters (???).

The twelve apostles - name them? - a trick question. The lists of the names of the apostles don't match up. Four are duplicates: James the greater, James the lesser, James the son of Zeb'edee, James the son of Alphaeus, Peter (Simon Peter), Simon the Zealot, Simeon, Jude, Judas, Thaddeus, Judas Thaddeus, Judas Iscariot, Judas Thomas, Thomas Didymus (twin, twin), Matthew, Andrew, Philip, Bartholomew, and John.

The Ethiopian Eunuch treasurer of Candace, a queen ruling in lieu of her minor son - A mystery: Ethiopians didn't castrate harem guards. Jews wouldn't allow a castrated man or a man with a flat nose anywhere near the temple (Lev 21:18), explaining David hated the blind and the lame (II Sam 5:8). And there was no Candace in Ethiopia at the time (Chapter 7 Ethiopian History, Understanding the Bible, Ray Shortell 2011).

Aretas - King of Damascus, father of Herod's first wife; after Herod's divorce, Aretas brought an army and taught Herod a lesson. Paul later visited Damascus with letters from the High priest to arrest any disciples of the Lord. Biblically tough to decipher whether Aretas or "the Jews" ran Paul out of town.

Gallio - Proconsul of Corinth (summer home of Caesar), who beats the chief ruler of the synagogue on Paul's behalf.

Mary - the sister of Mary (Jn 19:25)

Joseph of Arimathea of the Sanhedrin, Alphaeus, Clopas, Joseph, the husband of Mary - one and the same?

The brethren (at Rome) - greet Paul at Three Taverns. Were these Jews who had accepted Peter's worldview? Were these gentiles? Who might have been their evangelist(s)?

Hegesippius - Christian author of Antioch Syria 100 - 110. He writes about the death of James and the slaughter of Israel by Rome.

Eusebius - Christian author of Alexandria, Egypt, in the 300s - records the writings of Hegesippius and reports on texts of Josephus, which we lost to time (destroyed by Rome). The principal author through whom records have come, Eusebius authored at least 200 years after it happened, sort of like writing about the founding of America, now, and with him as our primary Church historian... Argh!

Origen - Early Christian author (185 ~ 254, p966 James, the Brother of Jesus, Robert Eisenman 1997).

Gospels - Mark - widely regarded as the first, suggested as Peter's scribe, Luke - widely regarded as Paul's scribe who also wrote Acts, Matthew - suggested as one of the disciples who was a tax collector or from Capernaum authored the prophesies Jesus fulfilled before any began writing gospels, John - suggested as one of the disciples. Paul's writings are considered source documents for the gospels, which came later. Also missing from the canon are the gospels of Judas, Thomas, Ebionites, and Mary Magdalen. The gnostic gospel of Marcion was widely regarded as heretical, lost to time (destroyed by Rome), but possibly pieced together recently through its refutation in later authors.

Appendix Timeline
4 BCE Herod the Terrible dies
6-7 Census of Quirinius of Syria
33 Standard year for crucifixion (three years after the fifteenth year of Tiberius Caesar during the reign of Pontius Pilate)
37 John the Baptist Beheaded
40 (my opinion) Jesus crucified (Jesus would be thirty-three after John's death, and Paul is not an idle man - Could Paul have sat still years while time was ticking?)
46 - 48 Famine in Judea - Paul sends relief per Acts
50 - 52 Paul meets Gallio, the Corinthian governor who is brother to Rome's Stoic Philosopher, Seneca.
60 - 62 Paul travels from Caesarea to Rome, meeting "the brothers" at "Three Taverns."
62 - James beheaded
64 - Rome burns. Nero fiddles and possibly restrains firefighters, blaming Christians.
66 - Tax rebellion begins
70 - Temple destroyed
73 - Masada falls
79 - Vesuvius erupts, covering Pompeii in volcanic ash
100 - 110 Hegessepius of Antioch
120 - Grandchildren of Jude seek Rome's approval for Judean bishopric and are hunted down and killed.

200 - Origen
300 - Eusebius of Alexandria

APPENDIX: CONQUERING DEATH

Understanding the Bible lists the quote: Romans ate the bodies of their gods in order to be greater than death. To me, at the time, this was apparent and obvious, since I've been to pagan Easter festivals where eggs as a memorial to the fertility goddess Oestarte were the ceremonial body and meal. Unfortunately, Oestarte and the Easter bunny, also indicating fertility, may have been a later addition to pagan worship and not from before the first century. The religion of Mithra that eats the body/sacrifice, does pre-date Christianity as would necessarily Paul's argument about whether or not eating at the table of demons is acceptable. The citation should have been: pg 237 James, the Brother of Jesus, Robert Eisenman 1997

SOURCES:

Cover – Elysian Fields – The Roman heaven as portrayed in the movie: Gladiator, 2000

Chapter 1 – Prelude: The End of Israel - Salt of the Earth
1) Temple gold paid Roman guards of Jewish slaves - Chapter 1 – The Power of Rome, Understanding the Bible, Ray Shortell 2013
2) Rome destroying the temple and blaming it on the Jews was a brilliant strategy - pg62, The Jesus Mysteries: Was the "Original Jesus" a Pagan G-d? Freke & Gandy 1999
3) It is unfortunate that we no longer have any of Marcion's own writings. They were deemed heretical ("false teachings") and destroyed. Forged, Bart D. Ehrman 2011.

Chapter 2 – Foreword: Understanding the Bible
1) Rome destroyed everything - Chapter 1, The Power of Rome, Understanding the Bible, Ray Shortell 2013
2) Samaritans on Mt. Gerazim 11,600 3.7.32 Wars, Jews of Scythia 13,000 2.18.3 Wars, Jews of Askelon 2,500 2.18.5 Wars, Josephus, William Whiston 1998,
3) [Josephus] retired to Rome… and spent his days writing… Introduction – Josephus, The Complete Works – William Whiston 1998
4) Chapter 19 – The Family of James – Understanding the Bible, Ray Shortell 2013
5) Chapter 3 – Caesar's Coin – Understanding the Bible, Ray Shortell 2013
6) Tax Revolt: Pg 375 James, the Brother of Jesus, Robert Eisenman 1997 and Chapter 3 – Caesar's Coin – Understanding the Bible, Ray Shortell 2013
7) Greeks/Trophimus/Herodians/Foreigners/Gentiles banned from the temple pg 544-545, The New Testament Code, Robert Eisenman 2006
8) Eunuchs/Circumcision/Mutilation – Lex Cornelia de Sicarius p922, James, the Brother of Jesus, Robert Eisenman 1997

Chapter 4 – Foreword: Timeline of Biblical Authorship
1) Daniel misses his own rulers: https://infidels.org/library/modern/chris_sandoval/daniel.html
2) Maccabeans inserted Ps 110:4 - Chapter 8 – Heaven – reference 4
3) Bible written in Babylon: 101 Myths of the Bible, David Greenberg 2000
4) Mark/Matthew authorship: pg 114, Eusebius, the Church History, Paul L. Maier 2007

Chapter 5 – Education Denounced by the Bible
(1) Sadducees – Temple Centered – pg381, James, the Brother of Jesus, Robert Eisenman 1997
(2) Tongues – p196, 206 James, the Brother of Jesus, Robert Eisenman 1997

Chapter 6 – Sacrifice: Human, Temple, Jesus, None
1) James: celibate, vegetarian & unshorn: pg 223 James, the Brother of Jesus, Robert Eisenman 1997 – Eating animal life dependent upon a proper sacrifice made by Righteous High Priests in the temple – pg 293 ibid.
2) After the fall of the temple not eating meat or drinking wine: pg 709 ibid

Chapter 8 - Heaven
1 – Resurrection first mentioned in Daniel – Appendix – Hebrew Bible Issues, Understanding the Bible, Ray Shortell 2013

2 - Per Pierre Krijbolder in Crucifixion and Turin Shroud Mysteries Solved 1976, 1999 p27 (Nathaniel – John Ch 1): This gift of G-d (Nathanael) may have been: the Essaean doctrine (insight) of the immortality of the individual human soul, whereas the traditional immortality of the soul was believed to be restricted to the collectivity in the form of a continuation of the individual's spirit in the (genetic) posterity.

3 - Moses was an Egyptian priest. The Egyptian g-d Horus may have been the origin of the word horoscope. Astrology professes faith in reincarnation with the soul progressing through one sign every thirty years of adult life - one degree per day with five interim days left over after the year is complete.

4 – In 167 BCE, Maccabeans used Psalm 110 to retain the high priesthood. "The Lord hath sworn, and will not repent, Thou are a priest forever in the order of Melchizedek." Robert Eisenman suggests Maccabeans as not previously of the priestly lineage (Postscript: Failed Messianic Prophesies, Understanding the Bible, Ray Shortell 2011). True to biblical form (Sadducean/Zealot/Dead Sea Scrolls/Essean too), Psalm 110 finds and expounds upon a previous reference in this case specifically to promote a non-Levitical priesthood: Gen 14:18. "And Melchizedek king of Salem brought forth water and wine: And he was the priest of the most high G-d."

5 - Dead Sea Scrolls, Mishnah, Talmud
- Check this book's chapter on when the Bible was written to find Paul writing before and possibly after the gospels, some suggesting the post-gospel writings to have been by students or forged.

Chapter 9 – Hell
(1) Jewish reincarnationists - http://www.chabad.org/kabbalah/article_cdo/aid/380599/jewish/Judaism-and-Reincarnation.htm
(2) Rabbis recount Mt Sinai as if all Jewish souls were there - http://www.aish.com/atr/Reincarnation-and-Dreams.html
(3) The Catholic Church may no longer profess a belief in Purgatory. My Grandmother, bless her soul, following the best known Catholic doctrine at the time taught us grandchildren of purgatory per her understanding of the Catholic faith.
(4) As one pastor put it: It's all fun and games until you burn in hell. Franklin NC LifeSpring Community Church

ABOUT THE AUTHOR

Ray Shortell attended the University of Illinois for a degree in Engineering (BS in Computer Science) and later pursued a degree in Physics at several schools in Georgia including some Master's courses while attending Roman Catholic churches St. Maria Goretti in Coal Valley, IL, St. John's in Champaign, IL, St. Andrew's in Roswell, GA and St. Michael's in Woodstock, GA. Additional time in prayer and study would be from the University of Illinois' Baptist Student Union's Inter Varsity Christian Fellowship (IVCF), the office prayer group, and the Church of the Nazarene in Marietta, Georgia with Elvin & Mary Frame. While going through this text, you will notice grave concern for biblical themes which deride education, study, books, the Jewish people, non-believers and generally any contradictory evidence (considered most important in the scientific method). Additional concern surrounds the later editing of scriptures there being multiple versions (ie. Mk 16 in the Catholic edition offers both shorter and longer endings). My personal conviction is that the violence (massacres) condoned by Moses, Joshua and David during the takeover of Caanan were reinterpreted to attempt to justify the violence of later religions using the books of Moses as a foundation. One Bible study which left me dumbfounded considered whether Israel's massacre of the children of Canaan was merciful in light of these otherwise growing up in a pagan society with polluted immortal souls. It might be questioned whether it is possible for someone such as myself holding such vitriol against multiple biblical themes to likewise hold a space for belief. My response as a Gnostic, which comes from a root word meaning "to know", is to say that everything was created for a purpose with nothing beyond the ken of our creator (Ps 86:13) or more concretely that with G-d all things are possible (Mt. 19:26).